976.9
EVD
Evdokimoff, Natasha
Kentucky
34880000823257

KENTUCKY

Natasha Evdokimoff

Published by Weigl Publishers Inc.
123 South Broad Street, Box 227
Mankato, MN   56002
USA
Web site: http://www.weigl.com

Library of Congress Cataloging-in-Publication Data available upon request from the publisher. Fax: (507) 388-2746 for the attention of the Publishing Records Department.

ISBN 1-59036-004-4

Printed in the United States of America
1 2 3 4 5 6 7 8 9 10   05 04 03 02 01

Editor
Michael Lowry
Copy Editor
Diana Marshall
Designers
Warren Clark
Terry Paulhus
Layout
Susan Kenyon
Photo Researcher
Angela Lowen

Photograph Credits

CONTENTS

Kentucky is well-known for its burley tobacco.

INTRODUCTION

Many people have experienced Kentucky without ever having set foot in the fifteenth state of the Union. Kentucky has lent its name to numerous world-renowned events and products, not the least of which is the exciting sport of **thoroughbred horse** racing. "The Sport of Kings," one of the state's oldest and most treasured sporting activities, traces its roots to the Kentucky Derby, a high-stakes horse race that the world has been watching every year since it began in 1875. Top-quality horses and jockeys come from around the world to compete in the Kentucky Derby.

Kentucky Fried Chicken, a chain of restaurants offering home-style fried chicken, was founded at a service station in Corbin. Kentucky is also the home of Fort Knox, which is known for its tight security. This heavily guarded military base near Louisville holds the nation's entire gold reserve within its vaults.

Horse racing in Kentucky dates back as far as 1783, when the downtown streets of Louisville served as a makeshift racecourse.

Kentucky has nearly 75,000 miles of roads and highways.

Getting There

Kentucky is one of the southeastern states. Ohio and West Virginia border Kentucky to the northeast. Illinois and Indiana border it to the northwest. Missouri borders Kentucky directly to the west, Virginia borders it to the east, and Tennessee borders it to the south. The Ohio River runs the entire length of Kentucky's northern border.

Getting around in Kentucky is quick and easy, due to a fantastic road system. The state has a large network of highways, including the state **turnpike**. Railroads connect most of Kentucky's major centers and deliver freight to large and small locations. Most of the state's railroads were built after the American Civil War. Waterways in Kentucky, such as the Ohio River, play a major role in transporting products in and out of the state.

All of Kentucky's major cities have airports. The Blue Grass Airport in Lexington, the Standiford Field in Louisville, and the Greater Cincinnati Airport in northern Kentucky are the busiest airports in the state.

QUICK FACTS

Kentucky is one of four commonwealth states in the Union. The word "commonwealth" dates back to the 1600s, when British settlers occupied the area. The other commonwealth states are Pennsylvania, Virginia, and Massachusetts.

After pioneers had settled the area, traders began to market the seed for "the blue grass of Kentucky."

Two men, a pioneer and a statesman, shaking hands appear on the state seal. They represent the state motto, "Together we stand. Divided we fall."

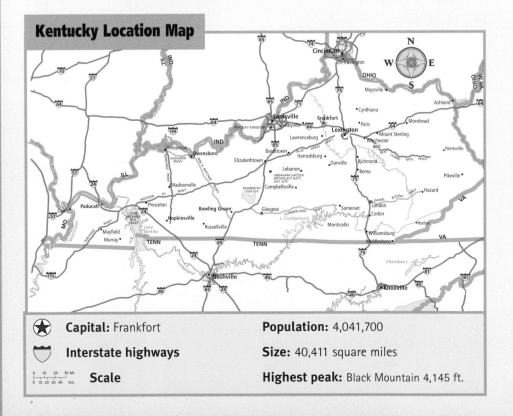

Kentucky Location Map

⭐ **Capital:** Frankfort

🛡 **Interstate highways**

Scale

Population: 4,041,700

Size: 40,411 square miles

Highest peak: Black Mountain 4,145 ft.

The Cumberland Gap changed hands four times during the American Civil War.

QUICK FACTS

The first Mother's Day was held in 1887 in Henderson, Kentucky, with the help of a teacher named Mary S. Wilson.

The state flag has a navy blue background with the state seal appearing in the center. It was adopted in 1918 and then amended in 1928, and again in 1962.

Kentucky is the birthplace of Abraham Lincoln and Jefferson Davies, who were opponents in the American Civil War.

The blue fields of Kentucky have been trampled on by the feet of many soldiers in battle. The Kentucky territory had only recently been settled when the American Revolution began in 1775. British colonists, Native Americans, and the thirteen American colonies battled for the land. In the end, the thirteen colonies gained control of the state.

The American Civil War had a special significance in Kentucky. The state was centrally located between the North and the South. Since Kentucky declared itself neutral in the American Civil War, its citizens were divided, fighting for both sides. Abraham Lincoln, born in Kentucky in 1809, became the sixteenth president of the United States in 1860. Lincoln played a major role in the American Civil War through his goal to end slavery in the country. He allowed slaves to join the Northern Army in the fight for their freedom. In 1862, Lincoln issued a proclamation that granted African Americans freedom from slavery. The war ended in 1865 with a Union victory.

Abraham Lincoln, Kentucky's most celebrated figure, has a statue dedicated to him in the Kentucky Capitol.

The city of Louisville was founded in 1778.

Since the days of the American Civil War, Kentucky has fostered the spirit of equality and prosperity. The state has created a vibrant economy out of the breeding and selling of thoroughbred horses, while maintaining the traditions of old-time country music, called bluegrass. A state of refined tastes, Kentucky is the only place where the Chevrolet Corvette, a luxury sports car, is manufactured. The state is also known for its high-quality bourbon.

A vast range of industries has helped keep the state's economy stable, from mining and natural gas production to forestry and manufacturing. Farm products also contribute greatly to the state's economy. Tobacco, soybeans, corn, wheat, and livestock earn agricultural income for the Bluegrass State. From horse racing to fried chicken, Kentucky has made a name for itself as a state of high-class sporting events and home-style pleasures.

QUICK FACTS

One of the world's most popular songs was written in Kentucky. "Happy Birthday to You" was composed by two sisters from Louisville in 1893.

While more than 400 horses are entered to compete in the Kentucky Derby each year, only 20 are chosen.

The selling of thoroughbred horses is an important part of Kentucky's economy. The record price paid for a 1-year-old thoroughbred is more than $13 million.

LAND AND CLIMATE

The landscape of Kentucky is alive with color from late September to late October.

The southern and western parts of Kentucky consist of rolling plains and jagged hillsides, where mint grows in abundance. In the west, there are **flood plains** that dozens of bird species migrate to each year. The northern portion of the state contains rich coal deposits within its rocky terrain.

Kentucky is located completely within the drainage basin of the Mississippi River. All the major rivers in the state flow into the Ohio River, which is a **tributary** of the Mississippi River. While Kentucky has no natural lakes, many human-made lakes can be found throughout the state, usually behind dams.

Kentucky's climate is mild, with warm summers and cool winters. The temperature varies between 38° Fahrenheit and 80°F throughout the year. The northern part of the state receives an average of 42 inches of precipitation, while the south receives an average of 50 inches.

The cave system at Mammoth Cave National Park is the longest in the world. Located just north of Bowling Green, it has more than 336 miles of passageways.

Kentucky mines produce more than 150 million tons of coal every year.

NATURAL RESOURCES

Kentucky is rich in coal and natural gas deposits. Each year, the state produces more than $3 billion worth of coal. Kentucky is the third-largest producer of coal in the country. It is mined from coal seams on the eastern and western sides of the state. Kentucky's coal mining dates back to the late 1800s. Back then, Kentucky coal was used to heat homes all over the country.

Mining was difficult work. Miners traveled deep into tunnels that were damp, dark, and covered in coal dust, which can be dangerous if inhaled. There was also the risk of the mine collapsing at any time. While coal mining continues today, machines now do much of the dangerous work. Coal has been ranked among Kentucky's most important exports for more than one century.

Kentucky's natural gas reserves are found mostly in the Big Sandy Gas Field, in the east. Natural gas is a clean-burning fuel that is widely used for heat and power. Gas wells in Kentucky reach as deep as 5,000 feet.

Kentucky's Portal 31 is a restored coal mine that teaches the state's rich coal-mining heritage.

QUICK FACTS

Kentucky has more than 100 quarries for limestone, clay, sand, and gravel mining.

Commercial forests cover about 47 percent of the state's land.

Kentucky has 12 million acres of forests. State lumber is used in the manufacturing of furniture and homes across the country. While oak is the most common hardwood produced in the state, hickory and pine are also frequently produced.

Kentucky's beech trees can grow to over 70 feet in height. Some are more than 300 years old.

PLANTS AND ANIMALS

Before settlers arrived in the area, Kentucky was almost completely covered by trees. Today, about half of the state's land is forested. Tulip poplar, American beech, white basswood, and sugar maple are just a few of the trees that are commonly found in the state.

Small plants also thrive in the state. Flowering shrubs, such as the azalea and the mountain laurel, are common. Many beautiful wildflowers, such as the bluebell, the lady's-slipper, and the violet, also bloom across the state. Patches of the state flower, the goldenrod, provide a colorful display in meadows and ditches every fall.

QUICK FACTS

The tulip poplar is the official state tree. It can live for 200 years and grow up to 145 feet.

The beauty of Kentucky can be enjoyed in any one of the state's fifty state parks.

The goldenrod is a native flower of Kentucky. It grows wild all across the state.

Fourteen species of azaleas are native to the eastern United States.

Kentucky's forests are filled with many kinds of wild animals. White-tailed deer are frequently seen roaming the land. Black bears are also in the area but are much less common. Smaller Kentucky creatures include beavers, foxes, minks, muskrats, raccoons, and woodchucks. Other animals, such as the red wolf, are being reintroduced to Kentucky.

Kentucky's trees are home to a variety of birds. Cardinals, blue jays, and chickadees fill the air with their songs. **Migratory** birds flock to the state to visit the flood plains, including catbirds, brown thrashers, cedar waxwings, and warblers. Game hunters search for bobwhites, pheasants, rock doves, and wild turkeys throughout the state.

Iowa once provided Kentucky with ninety-two wild turkeys to help its restoration efforts.

QUICK FACTS

Kentucky waters are filled with fishes. Bluegill, largemouth black bass, and catfish can be lured from state lakes and rivers.

The cardinal is the official state bird.

The state butterfly is the viceroy.

During the mid-1800s, Kentucky hunters trained dogs for particular hunts. Hounds were known as either gray fox hounds or red fox hounds.

Abraham Lincoln's boyhood home is located only a few miles from his birthplace, Knob Creek.

QUICK FACTS

Each year, tourists spend about $7 billion in Kentucky.

The first Kentucky Derby was held on May 17, 1875. Since then, it has been held on the first Saturday in May.

Each year, the state gears up for the Kentucky Derby with the Kentucky Derby Festival. During the 2 weeks leading up to the race, more than 1.5 million people attend close to seventy events.

TOURISM

One of Kentucky's most visited tourist attractions is a small log cabin. The cabin, 3 miles south of Hodgenville, is the birthplace of Abraham Lincoln. Lincoln lived in Kentucky until he was 7 years old. He later moved to the neighboring states of Indiana and Illinois before becoming the sixteenth president of the United States.

Churchill Downs, in Louisville, is a first-class horse-racing facility that attracts millions of visitors each year. The most popular race at Churchill Downs is the annual Kentucky Derby. This world-renowned event is attended by more than 130,000 spectators, many of whom are visitors to the state. Three-year-old Kentucky thoroughbred horses run 1.25 miles for the Blue Ribbon. These exceptionally fast horses run the race in less than 2 minutes. Derby day is a celebration of colors and sounds, as vibrant wreaths decorate the grounds, and bands fill the air with music.

The Kentucky Derby is the oldest annual horse race in the United States.

Chevrolet has made more than 30,000 Corvettes since the 1950s.

INDUSTRY

Kentucky's economy is supported by a number of different enterprises. Agriculture is an important source of income for the state. Although most farms in Kentucky are small in size by national standards, they produce around $3 billion for the state every year. Tobacco is the state's leading crop. In fact, only North Carolina produces more tobacco. Burley and dark leaf are the most common types of tobacco grown in Kentucky. Mature, green tobacco leaves are dried and sold to manufacturers across the country.

Kentucky is an important manufacturing center of transportation equipment. Sports cars, trucks, trailers, and airplane parts are made in the state. Chevrolet Corvettes, the popular flashy sports cars, are made exclusively in Bowling Green, Kentucky.

The size of an average Kentucky tobacco farm is only 4.2 acres.

Kentucky is among the nation's leading producers of coal.

Thoroughbred horses are the fastest horses in the world. They can maintain speeds of up to 45 miles per hour for a distance of slightly more than 1 mile.

Tourism is an important industry in the state, employing almost 150,000 Kentuckians.

GOODS AND SERVICES

Using its abundant natural resources, Kentucky produces a large amount of electricity. Coal-fired power stations provide 95 percent of the state's electricity. Water is also used to make electricity in the state. Large **hydroelectric** plants are found on the Ohio, Cumberland, and Tennessee rivers.

Kentucky's river systems are the state's gateways to trade. The rivers provide easy access to many big markets in the eastern United States. The major wholesale trade centers in the state are Louisville, Lexington, and Owensboro.

Kentucky is the nation's leading producer of thoroughbred horses. Horse breeding began in the state after the American Civil War. After Churchill Downs was built in 1875, and the first Kentucky Derby took place, the breeding of thoroughbred horses became an important part of the state's economy. Many colts are raised to become contenders in the Kentucky Derby, while others are sold to horse lovers around the world.

The 149-passenger Dixie Belle riverboat takes visitors on 1-hour-long cruises of the Kentucky River.

Kentucky is home to the nation's oldest printing house for the blind.

The first state newspaper was the *Kentucky Gazette,* founded in 1787.

Kentucky's first radio broadcast took place in 1922 from the WHAS station in Louisville.

Fort Knox covers 109,000 acres of land.

Those who want a college education have many schools to choose from in Kentucky. Close to 200,000 students attend the state's colleges. Transylvania University is the oldest university west of the Allegheny Mountains. It was founded in 1780 and named after the Transylvania Company. The University of Kentucky and the University of Louisville are among the largest universities in the state.

Kentuckians like to keep themselves current. There are numerous daily newspapers published throughout the state. Louisville's *Courier-Journal* was founded in 1868. It now has the largest circulation in Kentucky. Other favorite state newspapers are the *Lexington Herald-Leader* and Covington's *The Kentucky Post.*

Kentucky has a strong military presence at Fort Knox, near Louisville. Many American troops trained for combat on these grounds, in preparation for World War II. On the base, a museum showcases old army tanks, weapons, and some items that once belonged to General George Patton. The fort is best known for safeguarding the country's gold.

About $6 billion in gold is stored in the vaults at Fort Knox. These vaults are some of the most heavily guarded in the world.

FIRST NATIONS

Archeologists have found evidence to show that Native Americans have been living in Kentucky for as long as 12,000 years. Ancient artifacts reveal that several different Native-American groups thrived in the state. The Paleo-Indians were early hunters who lived in small groups, traveling the state's land in search of game, such as bison. Later, Native Peoples began to farm the land rather than hunt for their survival. They also began to make woven baskets, stone tools, and clay pottery.

Evidence of a Native-American group known as the Mound Builders can still be seen along the Ohio River. The Mound Builders created settlements on the tops of large piles of earth. The size, shape, and purpose of each mound differed. Some mounds seem to have been used as plazas and game arenas. Many of the mounds were used as platforms for religious structures or for the homes of important families.

Cornstalk, a great Shawnee chief, was the head of a confederacy of Native Americans.

QUICK FACTS

Most Native Americans left Kentucky after the arrival of the European settlers. Of those remaining, the Shawnee, Iroquois, and Delaware were the three main groups.

Many Native-American groups claimed Kentucky as their hunting ground, and they often fought for control of the land. The Native-American uprisings over land rights happened between 1763 and 1766.

In the 1700s, the Chickasaw forced the Shawnee out of western Kentucky.

James Harrod was one of the first Europeans to settle amongst Kentucky's Native Americans.

EXPLORERS AND MISSIONARIES

In the late 1600s, Europeans began to explore the Kentucky region. French and English explorers canoed down the state's rivers and trekked through forests in search of suitable land to settle. Colonel Abram Wood and Gabriel Arthur were two English explorers who ventured through the Kentucky territory around 1674. Father Jacques Marquette and explorer Louis Jolliet traveled down the Mississippi River in western Kentucky, for the French.

In 1750, a Virginian named Doctor Thomas Walker led the first major expedition into the area. Doctor Walker found easy entry into Kentucky through the Cumberland Gap. Once this passage was discovered, hunters and scouts rushed to the area. Daniel Boone was one of many "long hunters" who came to Kentucky in the early years. The name *long hunter* was given to any man who spent long periods of time hunting in the wilderness.

Richard Henderson became one of the state's original founders when he was granted 200,000 acres of Kentucky land.

QUICK FACTS

Doctor Thomas Walker was employed by the Loyal Land Company of Virginia when he came to explore the Kentucky region.

By 1749, many European land companies had sent explorers into Kentucky to survey the land and to stake their claims.

Daniel Boone was hired by the Transylvania Company to **blaze** the Wilderness Road into the heart of Kentucky, now known as the Bluegrass Region.

Daniel Boone first came to Kentucky in 1767.

Daniel Boone explored eastern Kentucky between 1769 and 1771.

EARLY SETTLERS

While he was born in Pennsylvania, Daniel Boone is known as a Kentucky pioneer. Boone came to Kentucky through the Cumberland Gap with a group of explorers known as the "Axe Men," for the axes they carried to mark the trees. Together, they blazed a trail through the wilderness to settle a fort, in 1775, that would later become known as Boonesborough. Boone noted that the land was fertile and would be good for farming. He was also impressed by the amount of game found in the forests. He quickly decided to stake a claim to the land.

During the American Revolution, the Shawnee, who were allies of the British, led many attacks on Kentucky settlements. The largest attack was on Boonesborough in 1778. Daniel Boone organized the defense of Boonesborough, and under his guidance the residents of the town defeated the attackers.

QUICK FACTS

Richard Henderson worked to colonize Kentucky. In a treaty with the Cherokee, he secured 17 million acres of land for European settlement.

In 1776, Kentucky was established as a county of Virginia.

Kentucky's first tobacco farms appeared around 1780 and helped to establish the state's economy.

In 1775, Daniel Boone was appointed to build a road upon which settlers could travel to Kentucky.

After the American Revolution, the county of Kentucky experienced a massive migration of settlers from the eastern regions of the country. The population quickly grew to more than 70,000, and with this growth came demands for independence from Virginia. Finally, on June 1, 1792, Kentucky became the fifteenth state of the Union.

During the early 1800s, as settlers continued to move to Kentucky, more and more wilderness was transformed into farmland. Tobacco became an important crop for Kentucky farmers, and by the 1860s, the state was the leading tobacco producer in the country. Horse breeders also began moving to the state when it was discovered that the fertile pastures of central Kentucky were ideal for raising horses.

When tensions developed within the United States over the issue of slavery, Kentucky tried to remain neutral. When the American Civil War erupted, neither the Union nor the Confederacy respected Kentucky's neutrality, and many battles were fought on state soil.

Captain James Harrod, along with thirty-two men, established Harrodstown in 1774.

Even in the state's early days, farming was an important industry.

QUICK FACTS

Harrodsburg was called Harrodstown when it was first settled. It was the first permanent European settlement in Kentucky.

During the first half of the nineteenth century, Kentucky's population grew by nearly 1 million. In 1860, Kentucky's population had swelled to more than 1.1 million residents.

By the 1860s, African Americans, who worked as slaves, made up close to 20 percent of the population in Kentucky.

POPULATION

With a population of more than 4 million, Kentucky is the twenty-fifth most populated state. During the nineteenth century, most Kentuckians lived in **rural** areas, many working as farmers. After 1960, the population began to move into **urban** centers in search of better jobs. Today, more than half of Kentucky's residents are city dwellers.

Even though the state is home to several large cities, Kentucky has retained its small-town charm. Quiet tourist communities and smaller college towns cover the state, giving Kentucky a pleasant and safe atmosphere. Louisville, including its surrounding neighborhoods, is the state's most populated city. Other Kentucky cities include Lexington, Owensboro, and Frankfort.

The population of Louisville is about 1 million.

Frankfort holds the Governor's Derby Breakfast each year in May. More than 12,000 revelers are treated to free food and entertainment.

The state seal was created just 6 months after Kentucky became a state in 1792.

QUICK FACTS

Another name for the state legislature is the General Assembly.

Kentucky's governor is elected to a 4-year term. The governor appoints other members to the executive branch of government.

Kentucky's Supreme Court is the highest court in the state.

POLITICS AND GOVERNMENT

There are three branches of the Kentucky state government—the executive branch, the legislative branch, and the judicial branch. The executive branch is led by the governor. It oversees all state dealings and ensures that state business is carried out correctly. The legislative branch passes new laws and has the power to remove old ones. The judicial branch is the court system where legal cases are tried. Kentucky has seven justices, or judges, that are elected to 8-year terms.

Frankfort is Kentucky's state capital. The city, which started out as a frontier outpost, is now home to the state legislature. The legislature is made up of 38 senators and 100 members of the House of Representatives.

The state's first constitution was adopted in 1792. Amendments were made to the constitution in 1799, 1850, and 1891. To make a change, or amendment, to the constitution, at least three-fifths of the legislature must approve the change.

Kentucky's State Capitol combines Greek and French architectural styles. It is the fourth building since 1792 to be used as the Capitol.

Bluegrass is the most popular type of music in Kentucky.

CULTURAL GROUPS

Kentucky has a rich folk tradition. The state was first settled by English, Scottish, and Irish immigrants. Descendants of these early settlers live in the state today and work hard to preserve their European heritage. Cultural festivals, such as the Highland Games in Glasgow, keep Scottish traditions alive. For 4 days every spring, ancestors of Kentucky's early Scottish settlers compete in traditional music and sporting events. The harp events and highland dancing competitions are popular attractions. Many of the competitors wear traditional Scottish kilts, which display their family plaid.

Bluegrass music is a unique feature of Kentucky's folk culture. A type of country music, it originated in the Bluegrass and Appalachian regions of the state. While bluegrass music typically has a fast beat and a strong rhythm, many bluegrass songs tell sad tales of lost love and loneliness. Traditional bluegrass instruments include the banjo, the bass, the **mandolin**, and the fiddle. Throughout the year, hundreds of bluegrass festivals are held across the state. Some festivals feature several days of non-stop music.

The Glasgow Highland Games feature competitions, dancing, music, and battle re-enactments that celebrate Kentucky's Scottish heritage.

Kentucky's Historic Shaker Village is the largest historic village in the United States.

Eastern Kentucky's mountain communities are home to many talented furniture makers and craftspeople. The town of Berea has more than forty craft shops full of handmade artifacts. In fact, Berea is known as the "Craft Capital of Kentucky."

The Museum of the American Quilters Society is located in Paducah.

About 8,000 Native Americans make their home in Kentucky.

The official name for the Shakers was the United Society of Believers in Christ's Second Appearing.

The Shaker movement began in New York in the late 1700s. By the 1840s, more than 6,000 Shakers lived in communities throughout the United States.

William Smith Monroe has been called the "Father of Bluegrass Music." He was born in Rosine, Kentucky, in 1911. Known as Bill to his fans, he played the mandolin for his band, The Blue Grass Boys. Bill hosted a popular variety show in the 1940s, which introduced Kentucky's brand of bluegrass music to the world.

The Shakers were once a distinct **communal** society in Kentucky. This religious group settled in the state during the late 1700s. The Shakers believed that they could become closer to their god through intense prayer. They held lengthy meetings and often became so involved in their prayers that they shook, which is how their name originated. The Shakers were well-known for their labor-saving inventions, such as the flat broom. In the late 1800s, the group slowly began to disappear. Today, tourists can visit Historic Shaker Village, in Pleasant Hill. This re-created village is dedicated to the memory of one of Kentucky's most peaceful and practical communities.

The Folklife Festival celebrates the folk arts and traditions of Kentucky.

ARTS AND ENTERTAINMENT

Many popular entertainers were born in Kentucky. Perhaps the best known is country-and-western singer Loretta Lynn. Born in Butcher Hollow in 1932, Lynn is the second of eight children from a poor coal-mining family. She began singing at an early age, performing in church and at local concerts. Her big break came when she won a talent contest and was invited by country legend Buck Owens to perform on his television show. Soon, she had a record deal of her own, marking the beginning of her musical journey. Lynn was the first female country-and-western artist to receive a gold album.

The Everly Brothers were a popular Kentucky music duo in the 1950s. Don Everly was born in Brownie in 1937, and his brother Phil was born in the same town in 1938. Their rock-and-roll songs "Bye-bye Love" and "Wake Up, Little Susie" turned them into nationally successful entertainers.

Country Music Highway was named after the many country musicians who were born in Kentucky.

QUICK FACTS

Loretta Lynn's autobiography, *Coal Miner's Daughter*, was made into an Academy Award-winning movie.

The Everly Brothers' early style of rock-and-roll influenced countless bands, including The Beatles and Simon and Garfunkel.

Kentucky folk art is recognized around the world for the quality of its craftsmanship. Kentucky crafts, such as quilts, furniture, and pottery, are considered works of art and can be found on display in museums and galleries throughout the state.

Kentucky arts and crafts, such as pottery, can be found in stores around the world.

QUICK FACTS

The Kentucky Center for the Arts hosts a variety of performing arts, including music concerts, theater productions, and dance performances.

During summer months, parks around the state stage outdoor plays.

Broadway shows are performed at the Lexington Opera House.

Theater productions have played an important role in Kentucky's entertainment scene for many years. Kentucky's first traveling theater group started more than 200 years ago. They were a diverse group of entertainers who danced, played music, and performed **acrobatic feats** to the delight of audiences across the state. The state's first community theater company was founded in Lexington in 1811. Luke Usher, a professionally trained actor known for his work in Shakespearean plays, was the founder. Today, audiences enjoy live theater throughout the state. Kentucky's rich history has been the inspiration for countless plays.

Classical music lovers attend performances by the Kentucky Opera Association and the Louisville Orchestra. Kentucky also has a well-respected ballet company based in Lexington.

Eben Henson founded the Pioneer Playhouse in 1950.

SPORTS

One of the greatest sports legends of all-time is from Kentucky. Born in Louisville in 1942, Cassius Clay would become the world's most renowned boxer. At the age of 22, Clay changed his name to Muhammad Ali when he became a Muslim. Ali's amazing strength and agility earned him the World Heavyweight Championship title three times during his career. Ali dominated the sport of boxing for more than two decades.

Another popular **equestrian** sport in Kentucky is eventing. Eventing competitions test horses and riders in three areas—**dressage**, cross-country riding, and show jumping. The Rolex Three-Day Event, held at the Kentucky Horse Park in Lexington, is one of only four top eventing competitions in the world.

Muhammad Ali claimed that his boxing style was to "float like a butterfly, sting like a bee."

The Rolex Three-Day Event is a complete test of the athletic abilities of the horse and the rider.

ROLEX

Kentucky has many caves and caverns for spelunkers to enjoy.

QUICK FACTS

Adolph Rupp was the head coach of the Kentucky Wildcats men's basketball team from 1930 to 1972. He led the team to 880 victories and 4 championships during his career.

Agony Avenue and Corkscrew Way are two tight passages in Kentucky caves.

Pennyrile Forest State Park, Kentucky Lake, and Cumberland Falls State Park are just three of the state's popular outdoor recreation locations.

Kentucky is the perfect place for those who love the outdoors. Spots for camping, hiking, horseback riding, and biking are plentiful in the state. Water sports are enjoyed at many of Kentucky's lakes and reservoirs. The state's dense forests are ideal for hunting, while fishers take advantage of the well-stocked rivers and streams. Kentucky is also known for its deep caves. Cave explorers, or spelunkers, probe into the damp darkness in search of interesting rock formations. Many of Kentucky's caves are hundreds of thousands of years old.

Kentuckians are fans of college sports. Basketball is one of the most popular college sports in the state. The universities of Louisville, Kentucky, and Kentucky Wesleyan have legions of faithful fans for their hoop-shooting teams. Kentucky's strong fan base attracts some of the best players and coaches to the state's university and college teams. As a result, Kentucky's basketball teams have enjoyed season after season of success. The University of Kentucky Wildcats men's basketball team has won seven national championship titles.

Kentucky schools have an impressive basketball tradition.

Brain Teasers

1

What is believed to be the inspiration behind Kentucky's state song?

Answer: Stephen Foster, the composer, is said to have been visiting his cousin near Bardstown, Kentucky, when inspiration struck. He was so overwhelmed by the beauty of the house and area that he wrote "My Old Kentucky Home."

2

Which popular sandwich was first served in Kentucky?

Answer: The world's first cheeseburger was served in Louisville, in 1934.

3

Who were Kentucky's first female settlers?

Answer: Rebecca and Jemima Boone, the wife and daughter of Daniel Boone, first arrived in Kentucky in 1775.

4

What is unusual about the fish, beetles, and crayfish found in Kentucky's caves?

Answer: Like many creatures that live in darkness, these cave-dwelling creatures are blind.

5 Which state tree is named after a beverage?

Answer: The Kentucky coffee tree. Early settlers gave the tree its name after they brewed the tree's seeds to make a hot drink.

6 Which Kentucky town is built within a meteor crater?

Answer: Middlesboro. It is the only town in the United States to be built inside a meteor crater.

7 When did the first thoroughbred horse arrive in Kentucky?

Answer: 1779. The first thoroughbred horse arrived 13 years before Kentucky became an official state.

8 What color is the Kentucky moon?

Answer: Blue. In 1940, Bill Monroe wrote the popular bluegrass song "Blue Moon of Kentucky."

FOR MORE INFORMATION

Books

Cary, Barbara. *Meet Abraham Lincoln*. Landmark Books Series. New York: Random House Children's Publishing, 2001.

Doolittle, William. *The Kentucky Derby: Run for the Roses*. Alexandria, VA: Time Life, 1999.

Trischka, Tony. *Teach Yourself Bluegrass Banjo*. New York: Music Sales Corporation, 1999.

Web Sites

You can also go online and have a look at the following Web sites:

Kentucky State
http://www.kydirect.net/

Stately Knowledge: Kentucky
http://www.ipl.org/youth/stateknow/ky1.html

Kentucky Kids Project
http://www.fayette.k12.ky.us/kentucky/

Fact Monster: Kentucky
http://www.factmonster.com/ipka/A0108217.html

Some Web sites stay current longer than others. To find other Kentucky Web sites, enter search terms such as "Kentucky," "Kentucky Derby," "Bluegrass," or any other topic you want to research.

GLOSSARY

acrobatic feats: gymnastic moves requiring agility, balance, and coordination

blaze: to make distinctive signs, such as chipped bark or paint on trees and rocks used to mark a trail route

communal: belonging to a community in which everything is shared

dressage: the training of a horse to carry out a series of precise commands in response to signals from its rider

equestrian: related to horseback riding

flood plains: flat plains alongside a river or stream that flood frequently

hydroelectric: electricity generated by moving water

mandolin: a stringed musical instrument that has a pear-shaped wooden body and a fretted neck

migratory: to travel back and forth between locations depending on the season

rural: relating to the country

thoroughbred horse: a breed of horse that originated in England, known for its racing ability

tributary: a body of water that flows to a larger body of water

turnpike: a high-speed roadway or highway, usually maintained by tolls, or service charges

urban: relating to the city

INDEX